Making the Most of Being Mentored

How to Grow From a Mentoring Partnership

Gordon F. Shea

A Fifty-Minute™ Series Book

CRISP PUBLICATIONS, INC.
Menlo Park, California

Making the Most of Being Mentored

How to Grow From a Mentoring Partnership

Gordon F. Shea

CREDITS:
Editor: **Karla Maree**
Senior Editor: **Debbie Woodbury**
Production Manager: **Judy Petry**
Text Design: **Amy Shayne**
Cover Design: **Fifth Street Design**
Artwork: **Ralph Mapson**
Typesetting: **Illeny Maaza**

© 1999 Crisp Publications, Inc.
Printed in the United States of America by Bawden Printing Company.

www.crisp-pub.com

Distribution to the U.S. Trade:

National Book Network, Inc.
4720 Boston Way
Lanham, MD 20706
1-800-462-6420

This book is printed on recyclable paper with soy ink.

PRINTED WITH SOY INK

99 00 01 02 10 9 8 7 6 5 4 3 2 1

Library of Congress Catalog Card Number
Shea, Gordon F.
Making the Most of Being Mentored:
How to Grow From a Mentoring Partnership
ISBN 1-56052-546-0

Learning Objectives For:

Making the Most of Being Mentored

The objectives for *Making the Most of Being Mentored* are listed below. They have been developed to guide you, the reader, to the core issues covered in this book.

OBJECTIVES

❑ 1) To explore how a mentoring relationship can be beneficial to the mentee, the mentor, and the organization

❑ 2) To discuss the responsibilities of mentees in managing their own personal development and career growth

❑ 3) To explain the skills needed to foster successful mentoring partnerships

❑ 4) To provide guidance on building and maintaining productive mentoring relationships

❑ 5) To identify techniques for maximizing results and using new skills to contribute to the success of the organization

ASSESSING YOUR PROGRESS

In addition to the learning objectives, Crisp, Inc. has developed an assessment that covers the fundamental information presented in this book. A twenty-five item, multiple choice/true-false questionnaire allows the reader to evaluate his or her comprehension of the subject matter. An answer sheet with a chart matching the questions to the listed objectives is also available. To learn how to obtain a copy of this assessment please call: 1-800-442-7477 and ask to speak with a Customer Service Representative.

Assessments should not be used in any selection process.

98644

Contents

Part 4 Building a Productive Relationship

Part 5 Maximizing Results

Part 6 Summary

Preface

This book is designed to complement my book *Mentoring: A Practical Guide*, also published by Crisp Publications, Inc. While *Mentoring* focuses on mastering the knowledge, skills, and practices of successful mentors, this book offers exercises, information, and self-study activities for those who would like to be mentored— "mentees."

The mentoring relationship is most effective when mentees understand that they are involved in a process which they can, and should, influence. *Making the Most of Being Mentored* lays a solid foundation for building this awareness and the skills that will enable mentees to achieve the maximum benefit from this valuable opportunity. The book also deals with practical aspects of mentoring, such as assessing what the mentee is able and willing to invest in the relationship and the challenges of various mentoring situations. But most importantly, this book confronts the common assumption that what the mentor does or says is the most important part of the mentor/mentee interaction. Actually, the opposite is true. The value of the mentoring partnership is determined by what the mentee does with what the mentor provides.

Mentors Help—Mentees Do!

Gordon F. Shea

Gordon F. Shea

About the Author

Gordon F. Shea is the author of 15 books and over two hundred articles on such subjects as: organizational development, leadership/management, communications, team building, and workforce development. He has published dozens of articles on mentoring in such periodicals as the *Managing Diversity Newsletter, Supervision, Women in Computing, Bottom Line Business*, and the *Commandant's Bulletin* (U.S. Coast Guard).

In addition to the 50-Minute™ books *Making the Most of Being Mentored* and *Mentoring: A Practical Guide*, Mr. Shea and Crisp Publications have collaborated on a best-selling training video, *Mentoring*, which demonstrates both sides of the relationship.

Mentor/Mentee:

A Special

Relationship

2

Three Basic Definitions

Mentoring:

➤ A developmental caring, sharing and helping relationship where one person invests time, know-how and effort in enhancing another person's growth, knowledge and skills.

➤ Responding to critical needs in the life of another person in ways that prepare that person for greater performance, productivity or achievement in the future.

Mentor:

➤ Anyone who has an important, long-lasting, beneficial life- or style-enhancing effect on another person, generally as a result of personal one-on-one contact (regardless of the media used).

➤ One who offers knowledge, insight, perspective or wisdom that is helpful to another person in a relationship that goes beyond doing one's duty or fulfilling one's obligations.

Mentee:

➤ A person being mentored by another person or persons; especially one who makes an effort to assess, internalize and use effectively the knowledge, skills, insights, perspective or wisdom offered by the mentor(s).

➤ A recipient of a mentor's help, especially a person who seeks out such help and uses it appropriately for developmental purposes whenever needed.

In this book we are focusing our attention on the role of the mentee.

EXERCISE

List below one developmental area where you might find it exciting, valuable or broadening to be mentored by an appropriate person:

_____

_____

Describe what such a mentor would have to know to meet these needs:

_____

_____

The Benefits of Being Mentored

Following is a list of reasons for entering into a mentoring relationship. Check (✔) those which are important to you.

❑ Benefit from another person's vision, experience and learning.

❑ Gain insight into the organizational culture, appropriate behaviors, attitudes and protocols and possibly receive special insider knowledge that is not generally available.

❑ Continue personal learning, performance improvement and talent development.

❑ Be involved in what's going on. Mentoring reduces isolation, permits access to activities and helps one serve as a learning link within the organization.

❑ Get help focusing on career plans and career moves.

❑ Remain mentally alert and valuable to the organization.

❑ Experience a non-threatening climate to test one's ideas, skills and viewpoints.

❑ Share an adult-to-adult partnership, a model of equals.

❑ Have a voluntary relationship.

❑ Become energized by achievement, mastery and personal growth.

❑ Grow in personal power and ability.

In some ways, the most important issue is that a mentee might, in time, be able to mentor other people—even being both mentor and mentee at the same time, in different relationships, for different areas of learning.

LESSONS ON MENTORING

Lee:

"I was hired as a cabling technician to do field installations for a high-tech communications company. Three months later Kevin was assigned to be my mentor. He said his job was to help me keep my skills up-to-date. He asked me what I wanted to become. I didn't know what to say, because to me a job was a job as long as I got paid enough. He said that my skills would be outdated in six to eighteen months and I'd eventually be unemployed if I didn't invest in myself. That scared me, so I said that though I wanted to learn, I didn't know how to plan a career.

"He had me fill out several paper instruments to provide feedback about myself and my abilities, inclinations and strengths. After we reviewed the results, he introduced me to several people who had also done cabling but had gone on to more complex and better-paying work. Now I'm enrolled in my second computer language certification course and have come to believe that education is a never-ending process."

Avery:

"I was hired and trained as a bank teller right out of high school. I liked the work well enough, but most of my co-workers had been tellers for years and I felt as if I were stuck. I mentioned this to a senior customer service rep and she asked me what I was going to do about it. She said if I didn't take charge of my own future other people would. I was flustered. I had assumed that if I worked hard I'd eventually get ahead in the organization. 'That's the way it used to be, but now you have to chart your own course,' she said. In time she started to counsel me on career planning. She became my mentor."

EXERCISE

Relate one situation where you started to change your attitude, behavior or values based on discussions you have had with another person:

_____

_____

_____

_____

How do you think the situation might have turned out if you hadn't had this person's help?

_____

_____

_____

_____

Mentoring: from the Machine Age...

Mentoring is a developmental art that is experiencing considerable change and new opportunity as society moves far away from the machine age.

The machine-age organization was characterized by:

➤ A many-layered, hierarchical structure that concentrated power and authority at the top

➤ Slow and difficult decision-making procedures, often with many sign-off steps

➤ Decisions made at the top without adequate knowledge of, or concern for, organization-wide consequences

➤ All "real" thinking and decision making was reserved for staff experts or managers

➤ The common assumption that "up in the organization" was the only way to go

➤ That it was only the stars that needed to be mentored

➤ The belief that "insider information" was the essential factor in getting ahead

➤ The assumption that any manager/executive had the "insider information" and therefore the qualifications to be a mentor

➤ A focus on career development rather than organization development

EXERCISE

If you have ever worked in such an organization, what were some of your experiences?

_____

_____

If you received mentoring, what was the outcome for you?

_____

_____

…to the Information Age

Just as with many other aspects of the emerging information-age, we may need to replace some of our outdated beliefs, behaviors and attitudes. In their place we must adopt some new realities, develop new skills and learn to cope with frequent changes in our work and personal environments. New forms and practices of mentoring can help us adapt in positive and constructive ways.

The information-age organization is characterized by:

➤ Fewer layers of management (flatter)

➤ A more flexible, adaptive and change-oriented environment

➤ Mentoring as a workforce development tool, a career-planning instrument, and a personal-enhancement asset

➤ More decision making by those closest to the customer

➤ The need to solicit and support ideas from the bottom up and across all organizational sectors

➤ Mechanisms to speed the flow of skills, knowledge and ideas from the point of origin to where they are needed

➤ Appreciation and use of diverse skills and viewpoints

➤ A need for mentors with different areas of expertise and the ability to meet different mentee needs

➤ A more democratic approach to developing people throughout the organization

EXERCISE

Can you identify one or more organizations noted for the above characteristics?

_____

_____

What would be the most significant benefit, to you, of being a mentee in an information-age organization?

_____

_____

A Growing Trend

Corporate recruiters report that would-be job applicants, particularly for high-tech firms, are asking if their prospective employers have a mentoring program. Years ago such a question would have been most unlikely, yet today it seems quite sensible.

Young people say they want to do good work—work that is interesting, challenging, and will keep their skills up to date. When a given technology can become obsolete in six to eighteen months, guided, focused learning is essential. Mentoring is often seen as a way to stay current professionally, to keep in touch with what is going on in the organization, and to make an important contribution through individual and team efforts.

In today's downsized, delayered and re-engineered (lean) organizations, many employees feel the need for personal contact with others whom they can trust and learn from. The shock of abandonment (downsizing) and the end of the assumption of lifetime employment have heightened their awareness of these needs. Being mentored can help meet those needs.

In the past, mentoring often just happened because an affinity developed between two people. Such a casual approach no longer meets the diverse needs of a modern workforce. The need for more effective information flow, sharing of ideas and the dependence on teamwork make these mentor/mentee links more vital.

This emerging role of the mentee as a major player in the organization's development is based on:

➤ the emergence of new mentee skills

➤ the need for more involved, committed and responsible personnel at all levels

➤ the need for a deep, personal and trusting developmental relationship

EXERCISE

Why are mentees important to your organization?

_____

_____

Mentors Help—Mentees Do!

It has been said everyone who "makes it" has had a mentor. That may have been true in the hierarchical organizations of the past. Traditionally in mentoring, older more experienced and knowledgeable individuals took younger, less sophisticated people under their wing and shared tips on how to get along and/or succeed in a given culture, environment or organization. Frequently, this kind of information was not available in any other form to the person being mentored.

Such personalized knowledge was beneficial to those being mentored because:

➤ it helped to keep them from making mistakes

➤ it aided them in conforming to the expectations of the organization (or society) and improved their performance

➤ it paved the way to becoming a member of the inner club

➤ it gave them access to those in power

Despite its value, this elitist system has lost favor in our society because it spawned favoritism, discrimination and a form of social cloning. Even as recently as a few decades ago, those selected for being mentored (often called protégé) tended to look like, think like and act like their mentors, who were mostly upper level managers. This protégé-style mentoring, then, perpetuated the values, thinking and behaviors of the past.

Today the mentee—a more neutral word and concept than protégé—is expected to be more proactive than in the past. The "new" mentoring is focused on what a mentee does as a result of the relationship and the mentor's help. Mentees can make much or little of their mentor's gifts. If the mentee doesn't change, learn and develop, the mentoring exercise has been of limited value. Therefore, the essence of an effective mentoring relationship is now led by the mentee rather than the mentor.

Above and Beyond

Mentoring is not:

➤ a training course

➤ a cross-training experience

➤ social chit-chat

True mentoring occurs when the participants go above mundane activities into something that helps the mentee transcend the ordinary, in a developmental sense.

A New Perspective

For most people, knowledge and know-how have always been very scarce, precious and hard to acquire until quite recently. Hiding or hoarding knowledge was common and was often the foundation of one's position, advantage and even the respect of the community.

Knowledge of a trade, of rites and rituals, or of an art or skills were not only rare, but usually took a long time to acquire. Consequently, the idea that the mentor was older, wiser or more knowledgeable became ingrained.

Much of that has changed, however. Available knowledge is growing exponentially and can swamp us. With the advent of computers young people often mentor those older. And, some mentors are helping their mentees to sort through the information overload and decide what—even good information—must be ignored. It is increasingly common to see mentor and mentee practicing interchangeable roles depending on who has the need and who has (for a given problem or dilemma) some of the answers.

The Productive Effects Mentors Have Had on You

When people talk about the mentors they've had, they almost always describe people who have impacted their lives in important, long-lasting and especially productive ways. These mentors often helped their mentee turn an important corner, opened new vistas for them, or helped them see themselves in a new and improved fashion. The experience or relationship may have been brief or extended, yet it was long enough to help the benefiting individual change and improve from that day forward. Your mentor might have been a parent, a teacher, a neighbor, a friend, or anyone else who helped you make a powerful, lasting beneficial change in your life.

EXAMPLE: ALL IN THE FAMILY

Diana was the youngest of six children. Upon graduation from high school, she expected to follow the family tradition where the girls married and raised children. All but one of Diana's siblings, Bill, considered high school to be terminal education. Bill had joined the Army out of high school, achieved a Bachelor's degree while in the service and developed a professional specialty that was transferable to civilian life.

The summer after she graduated, Bill engaged Diana in a private conversation. He said he was disappointed in her for accepting the family expectations for her future. He said she was too bright and talented for such a limited role in life, one based on sexual stereotypes as to what women could and couldn't do. The conversation, she said, lasted less then 30 minutes.

The next day Diana went out and joined the Air Force without telling her parents or discussing her plan with anyone. Now in her mid-thirties, she is happily married, has four children, is employed as a top-level Director of a Trade Association, and holds a Master's degree in Human Resources Development. Diana considers her brother's intervention just what she needed at the time—powerful mentoring. "With his help, I got to think of some options," she said. "I wasn't just following family tradition."

What Makes Mentoring Different and Special?

The key to mentoring is often the special effort, imagination, insight or awareness that the mentor gives—effort that goes above and beyond the expectations of the existing relationship.

Below are some factors which can influence whether an acquaintance, co-worker, friend or relative makes the transition to the role of a mentor.

➤ Mentoring requires a primary focus on the needs of the mentee and an effort to fulfill the most critical of these needs.

➤ Mentoring is often built on a just-in-time principle where the mentor offers the right help at the right time. A potential mentor must recognize when the mentee feels free to expose a deep-felt need, thereby enabling the mentor to provide the right help at the right time to the best of the mentor's ability.

➤ Much of what the mentor offers is personal learning or insight, which has never been written down anywhere. The mentor may not be aware of what he or she can offer until a mentee expresses a need or desire and the mentor realizes there may be a match between something they know and what their mentee needs.

➤ Mentoring requires going the extra mile for someone else. Many people may think twice about adding such a commitment to their busy lives. However, if they choose to do so, the rewards of personal achievement, mentee appreciation, and a sense of helping to build a better society can be enormous.

MY MENTORS: A QUICK CHECK

You have probably been mentored by one or more people but have not recognized it. Look back and identify some people who have helped you beyond performing their job or carrying out responsibilities (such as those of a teacher or parent). Write in that person's name with a one-sentence description of what that person did for you.

My teacher: _____

Who helped me by: _____

_____

My tutor: _____

Who helped me by: _____

_____

My coach: _____

Who helped me by: _____

_____

My counselor: _____

Who helped me by: _____

_____

My friend: _____

Who helped me by: _____

_____

My relative: _____

Who helped me by: _____

_____

Using the Power of the Mentor Role

There is a personal power source born into every human being. There are also a great many ways that this inner power can be disabled, suppressed, misdirected, and even crushed. For example, children who are undernourished, abused, traumatized, kept in ignorance, subjected to drugs (and so on), or forced to have their personalities distorted or curtailed in dozens of ways, might never have the power reserve available to them for building a happy, secure and productive life.

Even with a "normal" upbringing, there can be areas in peoples' lives that require differing degrees of help. Many mentors consider it their task to fill in the cracks in a person's vulnerabilities, provide what the person needs in the way of skill and insight and to empower them with what they need to build a better life.

In mentoring we see empowerment as helping others overcome their deficiencies, obstacles and disadvantages, so that they have a better chance to discover their talents and play their best game. How do mentors do this? By discovering what their mentee needs and doing what they can to fulfill those needs. Many times it leads to constructive life- or style-altering effects of significant and long-lasting consequence. It is not always easy, but it is less difficult than it seems to turn help into empowerment. The diagram below is an example of how even moderate assistance can really help someone live a fulfilling life.

Quality of Assistance

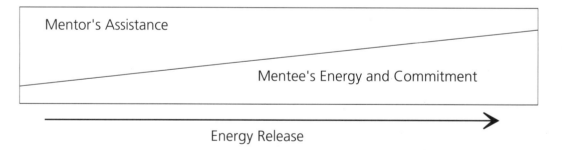

Note that the slanted line does not reach the corners because more than mentoring may be involved in a person's important changes.

What Mentors Can Offer

Mentors possess their own strengths and abilities that they offer to their mentees. These may include:

➤ Job or career related coaching and counseling that stretch the mentee

➤ Personal experiences and what they have learned or distilled from those experiences

➤ Access to a network of technical or business leaders

➤ Knowledge of emerging trends or developments within the organization or industry

➤ Assistance in developing and implementing personal development plans

➤ Perspective or contacts that provide cross-functional exposure, insight or experience

➤ Coaching behaviors consistent with organizational needs and values

EXERCISE

Review your own life experiences and identify up to three examples of situations where someone has helped you in any of these exceptional ways.

_____

_____

_____

_____

_____

_____

The Mentoring Investment

Mentoring is a qualitatively superior relationship. A teacher, for example, might spend the majority of time teaching, but also mentor one or more students, yet only spend a small percentage of her or his time doing so.

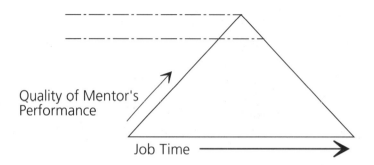

Therefore, several factors must come into play to achieve maximum results in the time available. Even formal, organization-sponsored relationships will not be successful without certain commitments by both the mentor and the mentee.

Playwright William Saroyan described a teacher he had in grade school who taught all of the students the same during class hours. However, the teacher recognized his special talent and tutored him after school on the use of language as an art form. He called her his "mentor."

Making the Most of the Relationship

Being aware of the following factors can help both parties have a more rewarding and productive association.

Mentees can help by:

➤ Being willing and able to share their needs with their mentor

➤ Articulating their needs clearly

➤ Feeling comfortable with their mentor

➤ Being willing to trust and to open up

➤ Choosing to develop and change themselves

Mentors need to watch themselves for:

➤ Having a limited network of knowledgeable and experienced contacts

➤ The need to improve listening or feedback skills

➤ Taking over mentees' problems and trying to solve them

➤ Giving advice, criticism or solutions

By providing information related to mentees' aspirations, mentors enable mentees to solve their own problems, and, as a result, motivate themselves to make things happen.

CASE STUDY: NETWORKING

Alexandria had worked for several years after her marriage as a buyer at a small retail company. Last summer she decided to move to another city and take a job in the purchasing department of a government agency. However, her rating and pay were quite low because her experience was somewhat limited.

Her new supervisor, Juanita, said that she would be pleased to mentor her if Alexandria would define her work-related objectives and identify specific areas in which she needed help, such as government procedures or laws under which the agency operated.

As Alexandria's supervisor began to teach her the essentials of the job, the two would meet for the last 30 minutes of each work day. When they started doing this, Juanita insisted that Alexandria share any problems she encountered on the job. Together they would work out ways to resolve these issues. At least 10 to 15 minutes of each meeting was centered on what Alexandria wanted to achieve in this and future jobs. The sessions were quite gratifying for Alexandria and raised her awareness of how complex it was to work for the government in this type of environment.

Just as Alexandria was getting her feet on the ground, Sandy, a co-worker, invited her to join the local chapter of the Purchasing Agents Association.

That same day she found an e-mail message from Dell, a purchasing agent in another region, offering to go through the purchasing process with her, step by step, and cover the exceptions as well. Dell said he would "help mentor Alexandria for success."

When Alexandria mentioned these coinciding events to her supervisor, Juanita replied, "It is no coincidence; we laid plans the day you reported for work. Your professional associations will also provide you with a succession of mentors as you successfully master one area after another."

CASE STUDY ANALYSIS

1. **What are some of the advantages of having a network of mentors?**

    _____

    _____

2. **Can you think of any potential disadvantages of having multiple mentors?**

    _____

    _____

3. **What techniques might Alexandria use to overcome any of the above disadvantages? (Hint: stress management techniques, establishing her own agendas for the sessions, etc.)**

    _____

    _____

4. **Alexandria agreed with Dell that their mentor/mentee relationship would be carried on via e-mail, fax and voice-mail, as needed. How can they use these tools most effectively?**

    _____

    _____

5. **What precautions should they exercise in using these tools?**

    _____

    _____

22

PART 2

The Proactive

Mentee

The Mentee as Partner

A generation ago, most employees were relatively unsophisticated, under-educated and frequently trained to be quite passive in the workplace—until and unless they achieved position power as a supervisor or above. Being mentored (if sanctioned at all) was reserved for technical, professional, or management personnel. In contrast, today's mentees may have mentors who possess fewer academic degrees or other attributes than they do. And a mentor may have less cross-cultural experience than a given mentee has. Yet such mentees can still benefit from the mentor's special knowledge, quality experience, organizational insight, or, perhaps, broader general education. It is also increasingly common for a younger person who has special know-how to mentor an older person who happens to need what the "junior partner" possesses.

Partnering

One dictionary definition of partner is: "a relationship, frequently between two people, in which each has equal status and a certain independence, but also implicit or formal obligations to the other." An increasing number of organizations are abandoning the historical "top down" perception of mentoring. They have found a sense of equality to be the basis for developing more mature, adult-to-adult, productive relationships. This allows mentees to be defined by the needs they have at a given time and the mentors by their abilities to assist in meeting those needs.

EXERCISE

Identify five problems you perceive that might arise in a "mentoring partnership." Think about issues that might be caused by difference in age, education, gender, experience and so forth.

_____

_____

_____

_____

_____

Attracting a Mentor's Help

When we approach another person to be our mentor, we are in effect asking that person to work for us, for free. Formal mentoring programs offered by employers, community centers, church groups and so on commonly provide the mentors—usually by asking for volunteers. The fact that enormous numbers of people *do* sign up to work, for free, reflects the goodwill that leads to helping relationships of various kinds (including mentoring).

However, people who volunteer to help others usually hope for three types of return for their effort:

1. A sense that they are making a constructive difference to their mentee's life

2. An occasional expression of appreciation or more frequent acknowledgment from their mentee

3. An enjoyable relationship

As a mentee there are several things you can do to evoke a mentor's interest in working with you:

➢ Know explicitly what you need or want from the relationship and have well-defined objectives

➢ Identify problems you believe might cause you to fail to meet your objectives (past, present or future)

➢ Have a clear statement of what you believe a mentor could do to help you

➢ Ask for no special favors above and beyond the limits of the relationship

➢ Develop a plan for reaching your objectives

➢ Build a high level of comfort between you and your mentor

➢ Be purposeful, pleasant and have interesting or challenging needs

In formal mentoring programs, the goals for mentee development might be set by the organizations. Personality types can be matched and required competencies clearly stated. Once a mentee has those items in shape, finding the right mentor is defined by their expertise or ability to help.

There are also times when you may want to recruit your own mentor beyond the limitations of the organization or program. In these cases taking the above steps will help you immensely.

Managing Your Own Self-Development

During the last decade or so, the accelerating pace of operations, the intensity of competition, and the rapid change in technology has led many organizations to decree that career development is a personal and individual matter.

This doesn't mean that organizations won't provide training, assistance and opportunities related to career management. But today's organizations define their corporate goals and objectives and expect employees to develop themselves in ways that support those goals. This approach means that the employer is no longer responsible for each person's development and/or advancement. In order to remain nimble and competitive, today's businesses must depend on employees who will take responsibility for upgrading their skills and preparing for their future. Mentees in particular are expected to be proactive in building their career.

EXERCISE

Write a brief paragraph describing how you might become more proactive in building your own career.

_____

_____

_____

_____

_____

_____

Self Empowerment Checklist

A successful mentee is self-empowered and takes action to get the most out of the mentoring opportunity. Review this list carefully and check (✓) the items that would be beneficial to your development.

❏ Learn techniques for strengthening personal health and wellness

❏ Develop win-win negotiating skills

❏ Use a system of ethical exercise and growth

❏ Strengthen communication skills (writing, speaking, listening)

❏ Invest time and effort in helping others (demonstrated caring)

❏ Practice team-building skills—bringing people to consensus

❏ Pursue deeper levels of job knowledge and skills

❏ Acquire and practice trust-building skills and behaviors

❏ Exercise to enhance physical strength, energy and stamina

❏ Seek ways to build personal empathy and better understanding of others

❏ Identify personal negative habits and reduce them

❏ Develop and practice assertiveness (versus aggressive) skills

❏ Practice sharing your ideas, skills and knowledge more broadly

❏ Learn and practice conflict resolution skills

❏ Strengthen one's character by study and application

❏ Apply a system for problem identification, analysis and decision making

❑ Master techniques for managing personal stress productively

❑ Manage one's time more productively

❑ Practice positive self-projection (in speech, dress, self-image, and so on)

❑ Seek ways to broaden personal vision and imagination

❑ Search for ways to enhance interpersonal sensitivity and awareness

❑ Relish and use positive and constructive humor

❑ Develop and repeat positive affirmations about one's constructive attributes

❑ Practice affirmations about an enhanced level of optimism and positive thinking

❑ Take initiative more often and generate the energy required to do so

❑ Other: _____

_____

Now select two to five items to focus on first. List them here and be prepared to discuss these developmental goals with your mentor.

_____

_____

_____

_____

_____

Determining Your Own Needs (or Wants)

What one person sees as a need, another might view as a want. One person may have a social need to work with other people. Another person might need solitude to think, to study, to write. Only you can determine which needs are driving you.

Needs and wants may intermingle and be difficult to sort out. Yet it is important to separate your needs from your wants since other people might not take your wants as seriously as you do. If you dig deeply enough into your wants, you might uncover a true need that is essential to your success and happiness.

EXERCISE

List three basic needs that you have (less stress, job security, the esteem of others, opportunity to use your talents, and so on)

1. _____

2. _____

3. _____

List three wants that you feel are important to you (such as a bigger office, the chance to telecommute, an expensive automobile, or to become a millionaire)

1. _____

2. _____

3. _____

For some people wants are simply an outlet for day-dreaming, whereas a need often provides a motivation that keeps us working until that goal is reasonably satisfied.

Intrinsic Motivation and Autonomy

Imagine Olympic Games where athletes win the contests but only their coaches appear on the winner's platform and get the medals. When employees are closely supervised, something similar happens—the supervisor gets recognized for "making things happen."

In the Olympic Games scenario, imagine the effect on the athletes' morale and performance. As you can imagine, the athlete's attitude would be, "Why bother if someone else is going to get the credit for my pain, struggle and hard work?"

Many firms now realize the value of allowing employees to make important decisions regarding their work. This leads to greater maturity, a self-driven willingness to take responsibility for that work and a sense of satisfaction that often is displayed as enthusiasm. Autonomy is the key. The ability not only to think or say "I did it!" but even more powerful, "I did it my way," or "I made a difference."

In many organizations, past adversarial relationships between management and workers (plus hostility and resentment over being treated as part of the machinery) kept many people from taking an active part in creating success in their workplace.

The issue of intrinsic (internal) motivation is critical. Our society is so focused on rewarding success with "carrots" and/or punishing failure with "sticks," that many people actually think they can motivate another person. In reality, they can only offer an employee a choice. In fact, the employee always makes the choice to accept or reject the carrot or the stick. High-tech firms in particular are tapping into the power of self-generated motivation instead of trying to manipulate employees.

EXERCISE

What would your work life be like if you were provided with the information, training and freedom to make more important decisions, thus stimulating your own inner motivation?

_____

_____

Becoming an Assertive Learner

Some people meet their mentors as passive learners. They expect to be "sponges" for information that will be properly dispensed by a mentor, who knows just what to say and do. This is not effective for either the mentor or the mentee.

Assertive learners focus on what they need to know and what they want to accomplish. They share their needs and goals with their mentor(s) as a first step in the relationship.

However, assertive mentees also gather knowledge and know-how, from other sources, which relate to the goals of their mentoring relationship. For instance, they may read reference material, watch appropriate educational TV shows, talk with knowledgeable people, search the Internet and even consult other mentors for input on the subject at hand.

The degree of investment in such a search may depend on the potential payback. For instance, a student teenage mentee in a community-sponsored "Stay in School" program might need to do little research on what he or she talks about with his or her mentor. However, a laid-off worker may need a lot of information if planning a career change.

EXERCISE

What are your learning habits? Are you a passive or assertive learner?

_____

_____

Describe recent efforts you have made to keep current in your field, to better understand the changes occurring in your employer's area of business, or to follow trends and developments that will affect your employment:

_____

_____

How much knowledge do you garner from highly knowledgeable people (i.e. potential mentors)? List some examples:

_____

_____

_____

If you have not been making much effort to actively learn recently, list two small steps you can take to get you back in the learning mode again:

_____

_____

Making a Habit of Life-Long Learning

We live in an extremely varied and complex world, with few limits to what a person can learn.

As a mentee, there is a great deal you can learn, as long as you take the initiative to make the most of your mentor's assistance. Raise insightful questions, do some research and homework, take the extra steps to make your mentor's experiences relevant for you. For example, if you are involved in a management development program, read up on the art of management. Invest in a program of self-study on topics relevant to your needs, desires, or curiosity.

Numerous studies have found that elderly people who are actively engaged in the learning process tend to live healthier, longer and more rewarding lives. In our evolving information-age, researchers have found that the straight-line life path, where we study for a number of years and then work, with only occasional updating of knowledge and skills, is not enough. We need to continue to learn useful and challenging material. This is illustrated by the Flexible Life-Plan Model which follows.

EXERCISE

Identify a few hobbies, extra curricular activities or pastimes that you have enjoyed and might enjoy as subsequent careers:

1. _____

2. _____

3. _____

Choose one you might like to explore more deeply. What would it be, and why?

_____

_____

What implications does the above have for your current career or a career you would like to pursue in the future?

_____

_____

Creating a Flexible Life Plan

A few years ago, organizations tended to discourage people from changing their career or even their employer. A person was expected to pick a career early and pursue it to retirement. Career consultants have described this *linear life plan* as the one most people have experienced.

Linear Life-Plan Model

In an increasing number of organizations, the linear life plan no longer fits reality. Since health is greatly improved, people are living longer, and because they often enjoy the work they are doing, many people are working longer. When we consider the volatility of today's workplace these consultants suggest that in the future a person may look forward to two, three, or even four careers in a lifetime. A flexible life plan is the trend of the future.

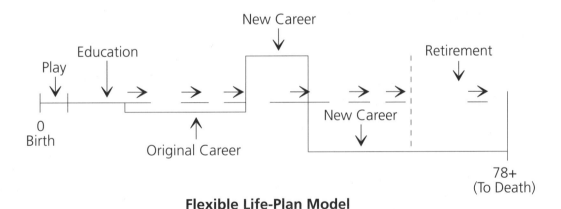

Flexible Life-Plan Model

Shifting Your Mental Context

A man faced a job counselor and said, "I'm a laid-off steelworker." This man only identified himself by his work and by his condition. Altering the way we define ourselves and our jobs, on the other hand, can lead to increasing our self-learning activities and new methods of problem solving. Embracing new tasks while abandoning others, or changing the environment in which our work is performed, can lead to a mental shift in the context of the situation.

Context shifting, that is, redefining the goals and tasks of a job, has been demonstrated as an effective way to help us learn. For example:

➤ It produces personal motivation to learn any material not specifically covered in formal training programs.

➤ It strengthens retention so that the positive effects of learning increases over time, rather than decreases.

➤ The person takes responsibility for reinforcing his or her own learning.

The pace of change in most organizations now is so great that entire positions can be eliminated or dramatically changed by a single technological advance. While this bothers some, it can be an opportunity for others, a chance to do something more interesting, more challenging and more rewarding. Today the watch-words are: personal versatility and adaptability.

EXERCISE

As a mentee, how can you enlist the help of one or more mentors to help you make your mental shift even more effective?

_____

_____

List three or four career options that might be reasonably feasible for you, and which you would find interesting and rewarding.

_____

_____

_____

_____

Staying Flexible

Managers have long claimed that "people naturally resist change." Nonsense! People resist change only if they see no gain from it or see some sort of loss or inconvenience from it. People embrace change that benefits them. Life is full of changes—some show gains, others loss.

Regardless, change usually involves stress. This can range from "good stress" (eustress) such as winning a game, to distress, such as being downsized out of a job. If stress in any aspect of life becomes too intense, lasts too long, or is repeated too often, it can cause physical damage. Thus significant adverse change may well generate resistance.

In an era when a technology or an occupation can become suddenly obsolete, the need to adapt successfully and quickly is essential. Increasingly, organizations are abandoning their search for employees who are standard pillars of orthodoxy and seeking out individuals who are versatile, adaptable and quick minded. These types are often referred to as *nimble*.

ARE YOU COMFORTABLE WITH CHANGE?

Place an "✗" on the scale to indicate how you usually respond to job-related change.

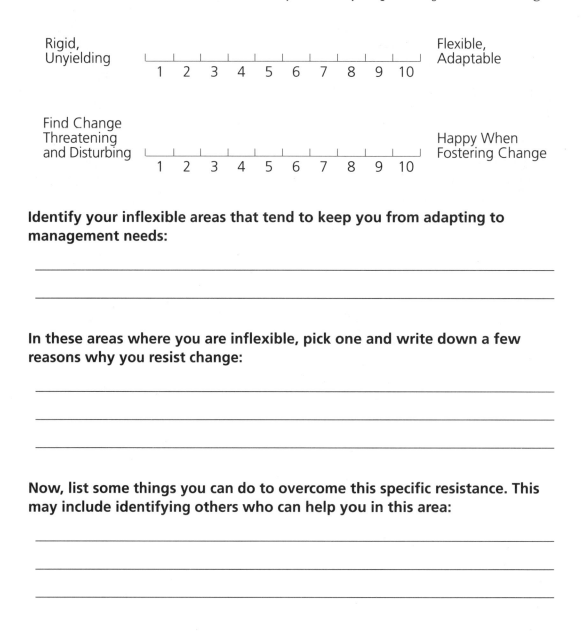

Rigid,
Unyielding
| 1 2 3 4 5 6 7 8 9 10 |
Flexible,
Adaptable

Find Change
Threatening
and Disturbing
| 1 2 3 4 5 6 7 8 9 10 |
Happy When
Fostering Change

Identify your inflexible areas that tend to keep you from adapting to management needs:

_____

_____

In these areas where you are inflexible, pick one and write down a few reasons why you resist change:

_____

_____

_____

Now, list some things you can do to overcome this specific resistance. This may include identifying others who can help you in this area:

_____

_____

_____

CASE STUDY: TURNING ADVERSITY INTO OPPORTUNITY

At 47, James was a Senior Design Engineer at a major defense contracting firm. He had worked there since shortly after graduating from college in his early 20s. Last Friday James was caught in the company's third wave of downsizing during the last six years.

The company offered those who were laid off a generous severance package. In these things, James came out fairly well, but he enjoys design work and had intended to keep working as long as possible. A week after the downsizing, James sat down to outline a personal "rest-of-my-life" plan.

The first thing James thought of was mentors. He had been assigned to a technical mentor when he first joined the company. The perspective, experience and wisdom of that man had provided a profound and beneficial affect on James's professional behavior, his sense of the engineering art and his passion for his work. Now, recognizing how much the world had changed since then, how much he had changed, and how dynamic the future was, it occurred to James that additional mentoring might help guide his future. He planned to take the following steps:

➤ Contact several design engineers who had been doing work similar to his who had found good work and good pay since leaving the company.

➤ Contact several younger engineers to find out what's "hot" in the job market and what he'd need to do to get current.

➤ Establish a network of mentors in his profession who could provide personal insights into the current job market and also refer him to other professionals who could provide specific assistance and mentoring while he defined his emerging needs.

➤ Identify career alternatives such as entering other fields of work, consulting opportunities, temporary work and moonlighting–particularly options that would expand his skills and knowledge.

CASE STUDY ANALYSIS

If something similar happened to you—such as job loss, greatly reduced income, the prospect of debt—and you decided to seek the help of some mentors, what would be the elements of your plan?

1. **What specific types of mentoring would be helpful to you under these conditions?**

_____

_____

_____

_____

2. **What types of mentors would you seek out? (For example, former co-workers who have been re-employed, people who could give you insight on how you might want to redirect your life or career, individuals familiar with changing attributes of the workplace, and so on.)**

_____

_____

_____

_____

3. **How would you approach these potential mentors to gain their assistance and support?**

_____

_____

_____

4. How would you state your need for help in such a way that it would be likely to gain assistance?

    _____

    _____

    _____

5. Given what you have learned so far about establishing a productive mentor/mentee relationship, what aspects of planning would you want to discuss with potential mentors? (For instance, establishing goals, expectations, agreements, and so on.)

    _____

    _____

    _____

Seven Special
Mentee Skills

Identifying Useful Mentee Skills

Until recently, little thought was given to developing mentee skills. Since most formal (organizationally-sponsored) mentoring programs were designed to prepare the mentee to enter specific types of occupations (such as technical, administrative, or managerial jobs), it was assumed that selected mentors from those fields knew everything the mentee needed to know. Mentees might be given a brief overview of the program, but that was about the only training they got.

EXERCISE

Identify any skills you think might be helpful to you in serving as a mentee:

_____

_____

_____

_____

_____

Discuss the above with your mentor, your supervisor, or even other mentees. Write down any additional skills they suggest that you have overlooked:

_____

_____

_____

_____

_____

EVALUATING YOUR COMMUNICATION HABITS

Advances in interpersonal communications have opened a variety of new options for mentees who wish to become more actively involved in their own development. Before going further, take a few minutes to take this communications quiz.

When meeting with your mentor (face to face, e-mail, fax, and so on) do you...

	Always	Frequently	Usually	Seldom	Never	Score
1. Communicate clearly						
2. Welcome your mentor's input (express appreciation or tell him or her how it will benefit you)						
3. Reveal your important feelings about the subjects discussed with your mentor						
4. Accept constructive feedback						
5. Practice openness and sincerity						
6. Take initiative to maintain the relationship with your mentor						
7. Actively join in to explore options with your mentor						
8. Share results with your mentor						
9. Listen for the whole message including mentor's feelings						
10. Be alert for mentor's non-verbal communications and use it as data.						

Total _____

Score yourself as follows: *Always = 10, Frequently = 8, Usually = 6, Seldom = 4, Never = 2*

If you scored below 70, you will benefit greatly by practicing the mentee skills which follow. A score of 80 or better means you are among the limited group of individuals who have good mentee interaction skills.

Skill 1: Ask Productive Questions

Rudyard Kipling wrote in his *Just So Stories*, "I have six honest serving men / they taught me all I know / Their names are What? and Why? and When? and How? and Where? and Who?"

If you can get those questions answered (and keep asking them as appropriate) you can learn almost anything. Unfortunately many mentees are not persistent enough in using them to probe more deeply into the learning opportunities at hand.

Since mentoring is not an adversarial relationship and is an attempt to gather facts for problem solving, an interrogative stance in using these questions is inappropriate. Used with sensitivity, these questions can be potent. Varied use of these questions can help your mentor get to the heart of what you need to know.

The quality of your questions can also make a difference. Open-ended questions, those that cannot be answered by a simple "yes" or "no," can facilitate a meaningful discussion. In contrast, a closed question tends to terminate a conversation as soon as it is answered.

Example:

> **Closed:** *"How many months will the program operate?"*
>
> **Open:** *"What level of commitment is expected for those participating in this program?"*

PRACTICE ASKING QUESTIONS

You have been given a lead from your mentor about a job opening in a part of the organization in which you would love to work. Using Kipling's guidelines, write down at least three productive questions to ask your mentor:

_____

_____

_____

_____

_____

Skill 2: Develop Key Listening Skills

Listening carefully is an art that is too often done badly. For example, many individuals miss the most important part of a message because they don't really hear the other person's feelings. In reality, another person's feelings may be the most important part of the message.

Virtually all human motivation involves feelings. Hearing those emotional drivers can tell us whether or not our mentor takes a given subject seriously and to what degree.

Before each meeting with your mentor, lay out what you would like to do, learn, or develop during that meeting. Know your subject as well as you can. Developing one or more written questions is also helpful for some people. Good listening skills will help you use your time together productively.

Here are four steps for improving your listening skills:

1. Listen for central ideas.

People often rely on examples, illustrations, and repetition to get their message across. By summarizing this information, you can get to the core of the message and focus more clearly on what your mentor is sharing with you.

2. Determine what is of personal value to you in your mentor's conversation.

Once you have clarified the central idea, consider how it applies to you. This will help reinforce the learning, since you can now better identify with the mentor's message.

3. Identify and eliminate as many of your "trigger" words as possible.

Virtually everyone has an emotional reaction, positive or negative, to certain words, ideas and associations. These "psychological deaf spots" often trigger an emotional reaction that may change your mood, set you on new paths of speculation, or otherwise prevent you from hearing the speaker's central idea. Work to overcome such emotional responses so you can be more receptive to what your mentor has to offer.

To become more aware of your trigger words, keep track of your next few conversations—with anyone—to see what words or phrases trigger an emotional response in you. Choose one and write down why you think it makes you react emotionally.

_____

_____

_____

4. Use the advantage of thought speed over speech speed productively.

Most people can think five to six times faster than another person can talk. The result is your mind starts to wander, you daydream, or you begin to mentally argue with the speaker. Unless you develop techniques for staying in touch with what your mentor is saying, important parts of the experience can be lost.

List two or three things you can do when your mind starts to wander.

_____

_____

_____

The forgoing does not suggest that you should suppress your feelings, but that you should use them to help define and solve problems.

Skill 3: Use Trust-Building Behaviors

Trust can't be assumed or commanded; it must be earned. Our behaviors can build or lessen the trust of others. Ponder each pair and identify behavior where you might strengthen your mentor's trust.

Compare each pair of behaviors listed here and on the next page.

Trust-Building Behaviors	Trust-Lessening Behaviors
Encourages	Discourages people; puts them down
Helps others	Remains aloof, uninvolved
Listens	Ignores, doesn't listen
Shares (opinions, ideas, thoughts)	Hides thoughts and feelings
Speaks frankly and directly	Indirect, vague, or devious in conversation
Consistent	Erratic, unpredictable
Cooperates	Competes, stresses winning over others
Acts as equal	Acts superior
Acts confident, self-assured	Insecure, fearful; takes lead from others
Accentuates the positive	Stresses deficiencies and negatives
Acts calmly under stress	Explodes, overreacts
Acts spontaneously and authentically	Strategizing, manipulative
Empathetic	Indifferent, cold, neutral
Fair and accurate in appraisal	Evaluative, judgmental

Trust-Building Behaviors	Trust-Lessening Behaviors
Gets close (physically or psychologically)	Remains distant; separate
Freeing and allowing	Controlling
Caring	Unconcerned
Friendly	Standoffish, uninvolved
Accepts and tolerates most behaviors	Critical, judgmental
Transparent, open, aboveboard	Covert, underhanded, sneaky
Conditional; open to new ideas and information	Convinced, close-minded, opinionated
Verbal and nonverbal congruency	Actions differ from words; sends mixed signals
Concentrates on resolving conflicts and interpersonal problems	Threatens, punishes, and acts vindictive
Empowers and builds people up	Cuts others down; insults, ridicules
Treats people as individuals	Categorizes and stereotypes

Skill 4: Overcome the Awe Factor

In many formal mentoring programs where mentees are selected and matched with mentors, some relationships are slow to get started. This seems especially true when mentors hold senior or highly-placed positions compared to the mentee.

It was discovered that in about four out of five such cases, the mentee showed reluctance to truly engage in the relationship. These mentees often failed to set developmental objectives for themselves, develop significant agenda items for the mentor/mentee meetings, or take any significant initiative during these sessions. Further, when the researchers probed, the mentees responded that they:

> ➤ were afraid to make mistakes in front of their mentors

> ➤ had trouble viewing their mentors as partners

> ➤ often considered their own problems and needs as insignificant

To make matters worse, these studies also showed that mentors tended to rate these same mentees as lacking initiative, as followers rather than as leaders, and as perceived poor performers. It was also discovered that in a year-long company-sponsored mentoring relationship, it commonly took three to four months for the mentees to feel comfortable enough with their mentors to begin actively participating.

Believing that "there are important people...and then there are the rest of us" can create a self-defeating self-fulfilling prophecy.

EXERCISE

List your views on how you feel about the possibility of associating with the prominent, the "well to do" or senior-level executives:

_____

_____

_____

_____

_____

If you are uncomfortable opening up to someone much higher in your organization, list a few resources you can use to help you overcome the awe factor:

_____

_____

_____

_____

_____

List some examples of how you can prepare for an intimidating meeting.

> **Example:** *"I will prepare a written list of questions before the meeting."*
> *"I will visualize us talking as if we've known each other for long time."*

_____

_____

_____

_____

_____

Skill 5: Resolve Differences

Hopefully it will never be necessary to actually confront your mentor for what he or she is doing or not doing. However, even in situations where it would be helpful to clarify or resolve differences, many mentees will be reluctant to take the initiative. Mentees may be concerned that they will not handle the situation well, they might be perceived as adversarial, or the relationship might be damaged and they will lose this source of important and useful information.

The Soft Response

One way to address questionable situations is to use the soft response.

> **Example:** *"That advice bothers me, but I'm not sure why."*
>
> *"That suggestion might be a good idea, but it doesn't fit my way of doing things."*

The goal of these soft responses is to invite a discussion of why the suggestion may not be applicable for you or why you might have difficulty carrying it out. This hopefully will lead to a greater understanding between the mentee and mentor.

"I" Versus "You" Messages

There is another, more powerful way to address a person's negative behavior that carries a low risk of damaging the relationship and is effective in gaining mentor change. It is called an "I" message.

The purpose of the "I" message is to focus on yourself rather than to place blame on the other person.

You message: *"You didn't show up for our meeting yesterday."*

I message: *"I had put on my calendar that we were meeting yesterday."*

The "I" message requires a great deal of thinking about what happened and reworking to frame the message in neutral terms.

An "I" message generally consists of three parts:

1. A non-blaming description of the mentor behavior that is giving you a problem. This description should be neutral, objective and journalistic in nature. Developing a non-blaming description of another person's behavior, when they have done something important enough to you to talk to them about it, is extremely difficult for most people.

    Example: *"In order to attend our weekly meetings, I drive to work rather than take the bus."*

2. A statement of the tangible and concrete effects on you, now or in the future.

    Example: *"Which means I have to pay to park near my office and then again to re-park after I return from our meetings."*

3. A statement of your feelings or emotions about what happened.

    Example: *"Whenever possible, I'd rather we rescheduled meetings a day in advance so I could plan to take the bus rather than drive on days we are not meeting."*

The above approach to addressing problems is almost always successful.

Skill 5: Resolve Differences (CONTINUED)

Working Out Problems

As in any close relationship, it is not surprising that occasional difficulties arise between mentor and mentee. It is helpful for a mentee to remember that the mentor is there to help. That doesn't mean that a mentor will solve problems for you, nor has to single-handedly handle differences that develop between you. The mentor doesn't have to invoke the no-fault divorce provision of the contract to cease mentoring. He or she only has to be less helpful than before (all the way to zero).

If problems are going to be resolved successfully, the outcome has to be a win-win one. This leaves both partners feeling good about the outcome and neither having an unfair edge over the other.

Characteristic of a two-sided conflict is that both parties argue rather than listen to the other person (except possibly to gather information that reinforces their own arguments).

In mentoring, one factor more than any other creates conflict between the partners: the belief among mentors that they should give advice. However, researchers in recent decades have documented just how advice-giving can place the mentee (or anyone else) into a difficult or even intolerable position. Advice can be productive if the receiver is so overwhelmed by a problem that they can't make a decision on a matter without engaging in years of study (such as grappling with the fine points of law, theology and medicine).

Buried in advice-giving suggestions are often subconscious statements such as:

> *"What I think you should do is to..."*

> *"I can solve your problem better than you can, so let me tell you how..."*

> *"If I were you, this is what I would do..."*

Mentees may resent or reject such advice, especially when they know that the advice is inappropriate to their situation.

EXERCISE

Describe one experience you have had with advice—from any source—that didn't fit your situation:

_____

_____

_____

List two or three words to describe how you felt:

_____

Did you follow the advice? If not, what did you do?

_____

_____

_____

Using what you learned from Skill 5: Resolve Differences, what could you have done to achieve a more comfortable outcome?

_____

_____

_____

Skill 6: Capture the Essence of Your Mentor's Help

Alertness, involvement and careful listening are all essential to successfully harvesting a mentor's gifts, whatever form they are in. But, how do you sort the necessary from the dispensable; the unusual from the ordinary; or the powerful from the trivial?

There are five specific actions that can help you capture the essence of those golden transactions your mentor offers you. These are:

1. Ask yourself at the end of each mentor/mentee meeting, "What did I learn today?"

2. Ask yourself, "How can I apply what I learned?"

3. Summarize for your mentor what you learned and how you will attempt to apply it.

4. Listen carefully to your mentor's feedback.

5. Ask questions about anything you experience in a given day that seems important to you.

Skill 7: Internalize Your Mentor's Input

Research in education and training suggests that we can process what we have learned more successfully if we follow this four-step process:

Step 1: Sort out the learning and find where patterns appear (you may do this with your mentor, another person, or by yourself).

Step 2: Review in your mind the learning (particularly the larger patterns) very shortly after they occur. There tends to be a substantial loss of detail in one to three hours after a learning experience.

Step 3: Record in a journal the outcome after each mentoring session, tape record or draw diagrams if appropriate and focus on anything useful to reinforce your learning.

Step 4: Discuss ideas, viewpoints and other attributes of the learning with another person. (You can also share with or teach another person what you have learned, if appropriate.)

It is not always what you have learned, but what you retain.

EXERCISE

How do you manage to review and retain what you learn from others?

_____

_____

_____

When you learn, observe, or experience something that is important to remember in detail, what techniques will you use to embed that learning in your long-term memory?

_____

_____

_____

PRACTICING POSITIVE BEHAVIORS

Below are eight behaviors that will help a mentee succeed. Answer each question yes or no. If yes, give a specific example. If no, think about something you can do, a technique to use, a behavior you can modify, or a resource you can consult to turn your "no" into a "yes" and record your plan in the space provided.

1. I set realistic expectations with my mentor/partner. ❑ Yes ❑ No

_____

_____

_____

2. I explore options openly. ❑ Yes ❑ No

_____

_____

_____

3. I search for ways to obtain goals. ❑ Yes ❑ No

_____

_____

_____

4. I follow through on any commitments I make. ❑ Yes ❑ No

_____

_____

_____

5. I learn and practice behaviors that enhance my personal inner power. ❑ Yes ❑ No

_____

_____

_____

6. I take initiative to keep in contact with my mentor. ❑ Yes ❑ No

_____

_____

_____

_____

7. I am proactive in a solid relationship. ❑ Yes ❑ No

_____

_____

_____

8. I take the initiative in creating (and amending) the agenda. ❑ Yes ❑ No

_____

_____

_____

CASE STUDY: THE FAGAN FACTOR

Jack was very pleased when he was assigned to be mentored by Nick in a formal mentoring program at work. Jack had expressed an interest in moving into sales work since he discovered that the company provided a great deal of training and that they also encouraged personnel to take job-related tuition-reimbursed courses in their field. He saw these opportunities as a way to compensate for his weak academic background.

Nick was considered a rapidly rising star—a young man on the go in the company's sales effort. Jack believed he could learn a great deal from Nick, and their early relationship seemed to bear this out. Nick seemed to be all that Jack wanted to be: self-confident, sophisticated, popular and at ease with everyone; as Jack saw it, a perfect role model.

Nick was eager to teach Jack the ropes of the sales game and to teach Jack what he called the "keys to the product lines." For the first two months as Nick's mentee, Jack alternated between feeling overwhelmed by the pace of his learning, and amazed at how much he had learned in such a short time. It even seemed that some of Nick's charisma had rubbed off on him. People in the plant began to show a respect and even deference toward him—something that Jack had never known before.

However, when Nick took Jack on some sales calls to other cities they partied with clients a great deal during the evenings. Jack concluded that his mentor had expensive taste. Later, Nick wanted him to pad his expense account and "contribute to the festivities." Jack felt uncomfortable with this and resisted. Nick got angry and said that Jack should carry his part of the load.

Jack began to suspect that more than padding was going on when they discussed some of the items for the expense account. Then he remembered several "private conversations" Nick had with some clients after he sent Jack on some errands.

CASE STUDY ANALYSIS

Fagan was a character in the Charles Dickens tale, *Oliver Twist*. He took street children into his quarters, fed them, gave them a place to stay, and taught them survival skills for 19th century England–picking pockets. Though some may have regarded Fagan as a mentor, he did not deserve this designation. By definition, a mentor provides beneficial or life-altering effects. In reality, many of the children taken in by Fagan would wind up going to prison.

1. **Assess Jack's options at this point:**

    _____

    _____

    _____

    _____

2. **Review your definition of mentor and decide if Nick is a true mentor.**

    ❑ **Yes** ❑ **No**

    Why? _____

    _____

    _____

3. **If you were Jack, based on what you know about this situation, what would you do?**

    _____

    _____

    _____

    _____

Building a Productive Relationship

Keys to Building a Productive Relationship

As we have said, much of what passes from mentor to mentee is personal learning. Therefore, mentors must be willing to share their experience, insight, perspective, and wisdom. In order to be effective, they must examine their own personal learning for applicability to your development. Mentoring can't be forced. If the mentor is disaffected or resentful he or she can simply withhold the most useful information, ideas and experience.

A mentoring partnership is never automatic. Successful characteristics, behaviors or attitudes have to be developed and practiced by each partner.

Building a productive relationship requires that:

➢ Each partner takes some initiative and risks

➢ The work occurs in a punishment-free environment

➢ Both participants mutually set agreed-upon goals

➢ Partners deal effectively with unmet objectives or expectations

Key Factors in Building an Effective Partnership

➢ Mutual respect

➢ Increased mentee productivity and empowerment

➢ Open mindedness

➢ Trust

➢ Reliable behavior

➢ Honesty and frankness

➢ Overcoming obstacles

➢ Commitment to mutual goals

➢ Finding common ground

➢ Mentor satisfaction

➢ Friendship (usually develops over time)

➢ Preparation for career competition

➢ Some values may need to be shared

Getting Started in the Relationship

Mentoring, like many important relationships, needs to get off to a good beginning.

Step 1: Communicate to your mentor what you hope to get from the relationship. If you are engaged in a formal relationship where management has set the objectives for the program, you may personally want to stress those objectives which are most important to you.

Step 2: Ask your mentor what he or she thinks are his or her strongest suits. Explore similarities between the mentor's strengths and your needs or wants.

Step 3: If you have no especially pressing needs to express or discuss, relax and enjoy the experience. Learn all that you can and look for opportunities to use what your mentor offers.

Step 4: If you find the relationship productive, you may want to continue it after the program is over. Though the mentor's formal help may no longer be needed, occasional contact may be helpful if you need someone to listen as you talk through a decision you may have to make.

EXERCISE

List any key items or needs you have which would be appropriate to bring up in your initial planning meeting:

_____

_____

_____

List anything else you would like to discuss with your mentor during your first working meeting:

_____

_____

_____

Establishing the Ground Rules

Many formal mentoring programs operate under specific guidelines, which might include any or all of the following:

- ❑ The relationship is voluntary (freely accepting the obligation or opportunities cuts out resentment or pressure)

- ❑ Mentor/mentee should not be in the same chain of command

- ❑ The supervisor of both the mentor and mentee must approve, if his or her "direct reports" are to be in a formal or organizationally sponsored relationship

- ❑ A mentor's guidance and counsel never supersedes that of the mentee's supervisor in matters that are the supervisor's responsibility

- ❑ Mentors and mentees must attend mentoring-related training

- ❑ The mentor/mentee partners mutually develop a mentoring agreement and adhere to it

- ❑ Both partners are expected to be actively involved in the process

- ❑ That there is a "no-fault divorce provision" where either party can end the relationship any time, for any reason (or no reason)

In many formal mentoring programs, management wants to make clear that they are not making promises of career advancement, protection from adversity or for special treatment. Check to see if your organization has any applicable ground rules for a mentoring program.

EXERCISE

Use the list above as a starting point for establishing ground rules by checking any to which you and your mentor agree. Use the space below to list any additional organizational ground rules that you are aware of and any others you and your mentor establish.

_____

_____

_____

Establishing Procedures for Meetings

Early in the relationship you and your mentor should establish operating procedures for meetings.

In most formal programs it is suggested that you:

➤ Meet once a week to ensure that a close relationship is established.

➤ Establish a meeting duration of somewhere between 30 minutes and 60 minutes for most meetings, so as to not unduly burden either partner.

➤ Decide who will set up meetings. Volunteering to do this can be a useful way to give something back to your mentor.

➤ Consider whether you should establish a formal agenda for your meetings. This may be beneficial for some partnerships, especially if either partner is inclined to digress from essential issues.

Key questions to ask:

➤ How often will we meet?

➤ How much time will we spend?

➤ Where will we meet?

➤ When: Over lunch, during work, or outside of work?

➤ Preferred day, hour, location, and so on?

➤ What do we do if a meeting has to be canceled or rescheduled?

It's a good idea for partners to exchange information on how to contact each other in case plans have to be rearranged. You might also ask your mentor if he or she has any other suggestions for getting the program organized.

The Spectrum of Mentor/Mentee Interactions

Mentoring relationships exist across a broad spectrum of opportunities.

Formal Program or Tradition	**Informal Relationship**	**Situational Responses**
Structured program to meet organizational (or societal) goals	Interpersonal agreement or understanding for mentor to help mentee, usually in specific areas	Isolated, specific acts by mentor to meet current mentee needs

Keep in mind:

➤ A mentoring relationship may shift or evolve over time and move along the spectrum as the partners choose.

➤ Mentees trained to function effectively across the total spectrum can adapt to a variety of individual needs and opportunities.

➤ A mentee may have several types of mentoring relationships operating at any given time with different individuals.

The Evolution of the Partnership

As shown by the spectrum on the previous page, mentees can seek out, or be offered, formal organizational support, informal help, or even situational (short-term) interventions in which no on-going relationship is established.

Actually, most mentoring relationships tend to evolve over time and be somewhat dependent on the power and value of the initial experience. Mentors and mentees often become friends, which means that in the future they can approach each other for mentoring on an as-needed basis. Such relationships can be long distance, last a long time, or exist for specific purposes.

Examples of long-term partnerships:

➤ Two members of the Coast Guard communicate by e-mail and the Internet even though they are stationed halfway around the world from each other.

➤ Two business people meet for lunch when one of them has a need to talk something over or explore new ideas. They have been doing this for over 30 years.

➤ An engineer has mentored technical personnel in informal relationships throughout his long career. He has been credited with greatly strengthening the company's technical staff.

EXERCISE

Do you see opportunities for extending a current or past mentoring relationship of your own?

_____

_____

What could be gained by keeping in touch with your mentor?

_____

_____

Are there any drawbacks to keeping in touch with your mentor?

_____

_____

Types of Mentoring Relationships

The characteristics of mentoring relationships will vary, depending on the nature of the partnership. Formal, informal, and situational relationships each tend to have their own unique traits.

Formal

Tend to be:

➣ measurably productive

➣ source of a developing relationship/friendship

➣ systematic, structured

➣ institutionalized

➣ on-going

➣ traditional

Are often characterized as being:

➣ driven by organizational needs

➣ focused on achieving organizational goals

➣ a method for matching or assigning mentors with mentees

➣ of fixed duration, based on goal achievement

➣ sponsored or sanctioned by the organization

Might include:

➣ monitoring of program

➣ measurement of results

➣ focus on goals of a special group

➣ specially designed organizational interventions

Types of Mentoring Relationships (CONTINUED)

Informal

Tend to be:

> ➤ voluntary

> ➤ very responsive to mentee needs

> ➤ personal

> ➤ loosely structured

> ➤ flexible

Are often characterized as being:

> ➤ caring, sharing, or helping initiated by the mentor

> ➤ a mutual acceptance of roles

> ➤ a path to developing respect and/or friendship

> ➤ dependent on mentor's knowledge, skills, abilities, and competence

Might include:

> ➤ mentee-revealed needs

> ➤ periodic assessment of results

> ➤ mentor having more than role relationship with mentee (supervisor, friend, parent)

> ➤ team mentoring with emphasis on one-on-one interaction

Situational

Tend to be:

- ➤ short, isolated episodes
- ➤ spontaneous, off-the-cuff interventions
- ➤ seemingly random
- ➤ often casual
- ➤ creative, innovative

Are often characterized as being:

- ➤ responsive to current needs/situations
- ➤ mentor-initiated intervention
- ➤ a one-time event
- ➤ the mentee's responsibility to use lessons offered
- ➤ not based on clearly defined expectations or outcomes

Might include:

- ➤ distinct, beneficial effects on the mentee's life or lifestyle
- ➤ network of mentors to call upon
- ➤ mentee's increased sensitivity to opportunities
- ➤ mentee assessing results later
- ➤ a memorable and lasting learning experience

MENTEE RESPONSIBILITIES IN A FORMAL MENTORING PROGRAM

In informal and situational mentoring, the relationship usually is quite free of structure. In a formal mentoring program, however, there may be external pressure to produce measurable results. Review the following list and check (✓) the behaviors that you feel will help you achieve maximum results from your mentoring partnership. You might want to share this list with your mentor; it will serve as an excellent tool to help make sure you both get off to a mutually productive start.

I will:

- ❑ Decide what I need from the relationship
- ❑ Strive to hold regular and frequent meetings with my mentor—weekly if possible
- ❑ Share my needs, goals, and desires with my mentor
- ❑ Follow through on any commitment I make
- ❑ Mutually set realistic expectations for our relationship
- ❑ Share failures as well as successes
- ❑ Be sincere, open and receptive to mentor input
- ❑ Accept graciously if my mentor is unable to meet some of my aspirations
- ❑ Initiate frequent and steady contact if appropriate
- ❑ Explore options openly with my mentor
- ❑ Share important feelings that I experience
- ❑ Invest myself in making the relationship a success
- ❑ Search for ways to achieve my objectives
- ❑ Be receptive to my mentor's point of view
- ❑ Mentally review, summarize and internalize the knowledge, skills and abilities I receive from my mentor—and make them mine!

Aligning Your Needs and Your Mentor's Abilities

We cannot reasonably expect our mentor to know everything and be able to do everything, or be able to answer all of our questions. Yet many mentees assume that because their mentor is more experienced, perhaps better educated, or has greater access to organizational resources, the mentor should be able to teach them anything or solve any problem they might have.

Like anyone else, a mentor has strengths and challenges. Most will respond to inquiries as best they can, based on what they have learned or experienced.

Mentoring is neither a marriage nor an adoption, yet relationships have foundered on unrealistic—or worse, unstated—expectations levied on one person by a partner.

Often these expectations derive from our cultural norms and are levied unconsciously. In a conventional marriage, for instance, a husband may expect certain conduct from his wife, and vice versa, without ever discussing these assumptions. A mentee may expect certain things from a mentor without ever making those expectations explicit.

For example, a mentee might inappropriately expect a mentor to:

➤ help the mentee achieve a promotion

➤ be an infinite font of wisdom

➤ advance the mentee's cause with the mentor's friends and associates

Any or all of the above might be contrary to the program's goals or the culture of the organization, or simply be unrealistic. Dig deep within yourself to discover your motives and expectations from any relationship, especially that with your mentor. Consider discussing these issues with other mentees; you may get some useful feedback.

EXERCISE

My expectations and assumptions of my mentor:

_____

_____

_____

Have you shared your expectations with your mentor? What was the result?

_____

_____

_____

When you have refined your expectations consider discussing them with your mentor. This can be an effective way to break through barriers if you feel you and your mentor are "stuck" and you aren't making any progress.

Giving Something Back: Balancing the Relationship

A recent study involved 312 mentors surveyed on what they hoped to get from the relationship. Often these mentors relied on their observations of what their mentee did and said about a given experience or bit of special learning.

The mentors said they hoped to:

"Improve my own leadership abilities."

"Experience the pleasure of helping someone succeed."

"Have a quality teaching experience."

"Enjoy the expression of a mentee's appreciation."

"Know that I am doing something important."

In general, responses to the survey focused on a relatively few, rather simple satisfiers. Yet one satisfier stood out above all the rest: mentors wanted to know that they "had made an important, long-lasting, positive change in another person's life, something that would help their mentees move forward into their future."

These satisfiers are what you give back to your mentor. It is in this "giving something back" that mentor and mentee become partners in development. To give back what the mentor appreciates means getting to know him or her very well. As the relationship matures and involves discussions about values, it should become clear what your mentor hopes to get out of your partnership.

EXERCISE

If you have a current or past mentor, describe what you believe that person would value most from you:

_____

_____

What leads you to the above conclusion?

_____

_____

Discovering Synergy!

Some mentors and mentees believe that the mentoring process is akin to magic. Some observe powerful, positive transformations in themselves, their partners or both. One mentor described the results of the relationship as "absolutely incredible, something like a religious conversion."

Others, with less zeal, are impressed by the productivity benefits and the warmth of friendship that developed and the remarkable changes that occurred in their lives. Both mentors and mentees report these kinds of gains.

While the mentor is supposed to give and the mentee to get, it often becomes a mutually beneficial process. The process of discussion, problem solving, and assessment of the results often leads to growth in understanding, skill, and perspective for both partners. Two people who really listen to each other, who work at helping each other, and who are concerned for each other, can hardly fail to create synergy. What grows between them is a relationship which is more than the sum of its parts.

In the current environment it is often the employer who benefits most by the ideas and improved performance of its associates. Employees in these programs tend to be more cooperative, more focused on beneficial results and less likely to get in each other's way.

The synergy that flows from mentoring benefits nearly everyone involved.

CASE STUDY: WHEN NEEDS ARE NOT MET

Genevieve received a medical degree from the National University of Haiti. With the help of her church she was able to enter the United States through an exception granted to immigrants who possess technical and professional skills needed in the U.S.

Genevieve took the standard U.S. examination for people who attended a foreign medical school, but failed. She was told that she was close to passing, but that English—which she had just learned in college—was her great weakness. This was visible on the exam by how she answered, or was unable to answer, some of the questions.

She quickly accepted temporary work in a local hospital as a technician, although language problems held her back. She believed that the opportunity to work in a medical high-tech environment would prove valuable when she finally passed her medical exam. Shortly after joining the hospital, she was invited to join a mentoring program, and accepted. She was assigned to Dr. Dobson's "protégé" program.

Genevieve had three primary concerns that she thought a mentor could either help her with, or at least point her in the right direction:

1. She wanted to be able to speak and write English more effectively.

2. She wanted to discover resources that could help her pass the medical examinations.

3. She needed guidance in how and where to pursue further schooling to become a cardiologist.

Unfortunately, Dr. Dobson most often took up much of the weekly mentor/mentee meetings avoiding her questions and telling long, involved stories about his own experiences which seemed to bear no connection to what Genevieve wanted to achieve. She suspected that it was difficult for him to understand her and that he considered the effort a waste of his time. One day she overheard him say, "She's one of those foreigners we've become so dependent on."

CASE STUDY ANALYSIS

1. Do you think this partnership is salvageable? If so, what steps might Genevieve take to get the relationship back on track? If not, why not?

_____

_____

_____

_____

_____

2. What could Dr. Dobson do to be more effective as a mentor?

_____

_____

_____

_____

_____

P A R T 5

Maximizing Results

Ensuring Balance in Your Life

People who are under excessive stress, juggling multiple obligations, experiencing financial problems, and so on are in a difficult position to constructively change themselves or the world around them. Many individuals who are in a tough spot try to get ahead by going faster and doing even more. This rarely works, as workaholics know all too well.

People need:

➤ Satisfying work

➤ Good health and wellness

➤ Financial security

➤ A feeling of orderliness in their personal or family life

➤ Good prospects for the future

➤ Some relaxation (including entertainment)

➤ Nourishment for their higher spirit

➤ Awareness of how the world is changing

➤ Good friends

EXERCISE

Identify three things to add to your own list of needs:

_____

_____

_____

How is the lack of one or more of these things reducing the time and/or energy you need to fulfill your destiny?

_____

_____

_____

Identify changes you are willing to make to achieve a healthy balance in your life:

_____

_____

_____

When this balance is missing, a mentor might be able to help. List at least two ways a mentor might help you.

_____

_____

_____

Identifying and Using Learning Styles

Researchers tell us that there are three primary ways people learn. However, each of us tend to have a preferred (primary) way to absorb information and skills. We often also have a secondary learning style that we find useful. Yet, we may have a deficit or lack of ability in the third learning style.

The three learning styles are:

Visual *"See you later"*

Auditory *"Talk to you later"*

Tactile *"Keep in touch"*

The phrases in quotes reflect how different people end a chat with a friend over the telephone. In casual conversation, these differences may not amount to much. However, if you get into the "How to Do It" stuff and your mentor has a primary and secondary learning style that differs from yours, it might cause misunderstandings.

For example, if your mentor is primarily visual, and secondarily auditory, he or she is likely to communicate with picture diagrams and maps. If you are primarily tactile and secondarily auditory, you might find you don't understand diagrams very easily. Your mentor also might not appreciate your need for hands-on learning. Learning styles should become a question both partners should explore early on the relationship.

Exercise

What are your preferred learning styles?

Primary:_____ **Secondary:** _____

These often show up in your schooling experiences or study habits. What did you use for clues?

_____

_____

_____

Pick a mentor or a friend and try to identify that person's primary and secondary learning style. What behaviors helped you decide?

_____

_____

_____

Diversity Issues in Mentoring

There have always been those who felt it was very important to give the newcomers a helping hand. Immigrants often lacked familiarity with the customs, rules and culture of their new homeland. A person who knew the ropes took the "greenhorns" (as they were often called) and taught them how to get along in this unfamiliar country.

As our workforce becomes more diverse, there is a growing need for mentors and a need to help newcomers adapt to the workplace as quickly as possible. But that is only part of the story. Mentees can learn several skills that will strengthen their ability to obtain, retain, and use more effectively the help their mentors offer.

EXERCISE

From what you have learned so far from this book, and your own thoughts, identify some benefits for preparing for the mentoring experience through special studies or training:

_____

_____

_____

Training is an investment in the person being trained. Identify some ways to make this investment in yourself pay off:

_____

_____

_____

Cultural Diversity: Gaining a New Perspective

Many people wish to work with a mentor they like, one who is friendly and with whom they can develop a rapport. This comfort zone approach may be very pleasant and productive, yet such a relationship may have the opposite effect and cut a mentee off from an optimum experience.

Some organizations have mentors and mentees take the Myers-Briggs Personality Preference Indicator (or similar tool) so they can match people with a compatible personality type. There can be a surprising loss if people are too comfortable working together as mentor and mentee. Compatibility between mentor and mentee might be helpful in some cases, but it all depends on what the mentee wants to learn or achieve.

In many organization, staff personnel often match mentors and mentees. At other times the mentee might search out mentors that can help; or the mentor just sees someone that needs help and pitches in.

We need to constantly acquire knowledge and skills to stay competitive. Therefore, diversity provides opportunities to build personal power. You can learn more from someone who is quite different from you in background, culture, religion, life experience, or whatever, than you may from a person who is quite similar to yourself. Dealing with this diversity of viewpoints can help both partners.

The best results from mentoring are often gained from the insights a mentor develops from his or her life experience.

EXERCISE

What might be some benefits to you of having a mentor of the opposite sex? How might the mentor benefit?

_____

_____

What might be some benefits to you of having a mentor from a culture different than yours (different by way of race, socio-economic backgrounds, religion)? How might the mentor benefit?

_____

_____

Overcoming Your Resistance to Change

Mentoring implies that you, the mentee, will eventually change as a result of the experience. Supervisors and managers who complain that people naturally resist change generally are doing something negative that causes others to be suspicious or hostile to new things. Three factors, if incorporated into the change process, can improve the likelihood that a proposed change will gain cooperation.

1. People need time to learn about the nature of the change and to internalize what they learn. They want to know the why of it and how it will truly affect them.

2. People want to influence or control change that affects them.

3. If the change is understandable and supportable, people will want to contribute to the process–to become part of it.

We need a certain amount of time and energy to adjust to change. While the effects of such stress can generally be reduced or managed using a variety of relaxation techniques, it is important for mentees to recognize the connection between change and stress, and take steps to facilitate change which will be beneficial to one's development. Some changes you may choose to initiate on your own.

EXERCISE

Describe situations you have encountered that illustrate the distinction between positive and negative change.

Positive:

_____

_____

_____

Negative:

_____

_____

_____

Overcoming Inertia in the Organization

The law of inertia says a body in motion tends to remain in motion and that a body at rest tends to remain at rest. When most or all of an organization is stuck in the past and not changing and adapting with the marketplace, inertia can endanger everyone's job. In traditional organizations people tend to avoid change because the organization avoids change.

Common reasons for inertia within an organization are:

➤ A desire to get the job done–as they see it

➤ Habit: no need for decision making and risk taking–why bother?

➤ Fear of the unknown consequences of decisions that produce change

➤ Past failures and fear of new failures (because failure is often punished)

➤ Concern for lack of time and other resources

➤ Fear that the change may cause failure in other areas

➤ Feeling that a specific change is inappropriate

➤ Implied criticism–change may be regarded as an indication that the change agent is not already doing what is right

Mentees can help an organization's efforts to adapt to changing conditions by:

➤ Projecting confident vocal support of productive change

➤ Initiating open-ended discussions about changes that are affecting similar organizations

➤ Looking for opportunities to join others in promoting productive adaptations to the changing world

EXERCISE

Describe two beneficial changes that could strengthen your organization. (No magic can be assumed!)

1. _____

2. _____

Avoiding the Power Game

In hierarchical organizations, many managers—encouraged by the use of the term protégé—often play competitive games around mentoring. Mentors sometimes use their protégés as pawns in power struggles, and sponsor their protégés' advancement without regard to merit of performance compared to other job candidates. Such mentors may focus on teaching their protégés the tricks of the trade, such as skills on how to sabotage their competitors (rather than how to develop their own talents).

Many protégés, not being foolish, decide that, if that is the game and how it is played, they will play it to the best of their ability. The result is that sometimes political talent outshines other abilities. As a consequence, mentees attach themselves to the most powerful or highest ranking mentor they can find.

While many organizations include a disclaimer of favoritism or special treatment, people who are heavily career-focused keep trying for gains. This creates a problem, since it is increasingly important that mentees take responsibility for planning and managing both their personal and their career development.

Avoid the temptation to play the power game. As organizations move to competency-based performance plans, employees need to demonstrate that they can achieve results and be team players. Furthermore, politically-based partnerships might prove to be counter-productive to the mentee's career in the long run. Accept that mentoring is, at its core, a developmental effort to build skills and understanding, not just alliances. Strive to acquire skills and knowledge that will help you achieve advancement based on your own merit.

EXERCISE

List a few examples of individuals, organizations, or groups that play the power game:

_____

_____

Do you see, or foresee, any long-term negative effects from doing this? What are they?

_____

_____

_____

Ending the Relationship

Mentees often want to know, "What do I do when I've outgrown my mentor?"

The obvious answer is to end the relationship. However, there is often a put-down indicated by the word outgrown. It might imply that the mentor has not grown according to the mentee's standards. In reality, the mentor has helped the mentee achieve his or her objectives. Therefore, a more fair response is, "I've gotten what I need and it is time for me to meet new challenges. Thanks for your help!"

This means a celebration is in order. Mentees should review the successes of the relationship by comparing what they now know to what they knew when they started working with the mentor. They should express appreciation for the mentor's time and assistance and for all that they have learned as a result.

Most people have complexity built into them in dozens of dimensions. In marriage, one partner might complain that their counterpart has not grown (presumably as much as they have) and therefore they have outgrown the other person. Such a viewpoint is often one-dimensional and even self-deluding. The real tragedy seems to be that one partner gets bored with the other and wants to split. This can happen in mentoring as well.

Unfortunately, one partner or the other is often playing a nasty game. The partner waits for the boredom to become excessive before sharing these feelings. By then the relationship is seriously damaged, and the "bored" partner walks away from it with a clear conscience. Such a tactic is manipulative and unnecessarily damaging to the relationship and the other partner.

Remember, mentoring relationships can be modified or terminated "at any time, for any reason, or no reason" (fault-free). There is no need to place blame in order to end the partnership.

EXERCISE

What are some ways you might revive a flagging relationship, or end it?

_____

_____

_____

CASE STUDY: THE PROBLEM WITH "STARS"

Only a month after graduating from college, Joe accepted a job with a federal agency in his chosen professional field. He arrived his first morning ready for work, but also somewhat nervous, since this was his first "real job."

Joe and eighteen other young people received a brief orientation presentation, including a film on the agency, its structure and mission. Each participant was also given a folder listing "all of the things you need to know"— including instructions on how to fill out time sheets, a map of local bus routes, key telephone numbers in the agency and other valuable information.

The big surprise of the day came when they were told that they had been singled out for a new six-month mentoring program where they would be rotated through several jobs and be mentored by the manager in each department that they would work in. They were also to be called "leadership interns," a new designation in that agency. When they were given the list of participants in the program, Joe noticed they were to be referred to as organizational "stars—the high-potential people expected to lead the agency some day."

Although Joe felt flattered by the attention he was receiving, he was somewhat uncomfortable when he thought over the agency's plans for him and other interns. His concerns were:

➤ He had a technical background, wanted to do "real work" in his specialty and didn't want to "spend six months wandering around the place," as he put it.

➤ He wondered about the reaction of other employees to his group now that they were being identified as "stars" and the fact that these individuals were to be the leaders of the future.

➤ He wasn't at all sure he wanted to be a "star" or even a leader/manager.

CASE STUDY ANALYSIS

Research reports indicate that individuals tagged as high-potential performers (and given opportunities and training beyond that of their cohorts) often prove disappointing in later performance. For example, in succession planning for bright young people, academic performance was the basis for inducting them into the program, though performance in a commercial company or in a government agency requires quite different criteria.

Joe didn't want to seem ungrateful, but he had three concerns that he needed to discuss with his mentors. Help Joe by coming up with some options.

How could he talk to his mentor(s) about getting out of the program and starting technical work?

_____

_____

_____

Joe felt uncomfortable about the elite group and being designated as stars. As new employees, none of them had _earned_ the designation of star. What is the message management is sending to the non-stars? Joe looked up star in his pocket dictionary: "To shine as a star; to appear as an eminent actor among inferior players."

What, if anything, should Joe do about this?

_____

_____

_____

Joe also had his sights set on a different kind of career path—what should he do about this?

_____

_____

_____

Summary

Participating in the Organization of the Future

As we move into the twenty-first century, we find most organizations have undergone more change in the past decade than they have in the previous hundred years. The old hierarchy with its tight span of control and layer after layer of managers is obsolete.

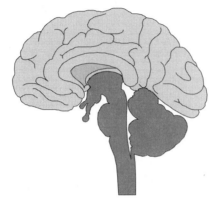

The New Organization Chart

The new organization will increasingly look like the above chart. What is it?

It is an organizational chart without the vertical structure of boxes in a pyramidal form with which we are so familiar. It is a picture of the human brain.

The organization of the future functions much like the human brain. For example, front-line employees may sense a change in the environment, customer preferences, or important technological change. Just like sense organs, they send messages to those parts of the organization affected by the changes. Those circuits assess the implications of the change, as to what parts and to what degree adjustments must be made, then the data banks provide information related to all existing aspects of the change. The information is finally routed to those employees best suited to decide how to handle the change. Once a successful response is made, that series of actions becomes part of the organization's data bank and the organization is ready for its next challenge. The traditional, many-layered chain of command is too slow in response to change. We need new models of organization to ensure that we fully utilize individual talents and the synergy of team work. Mentoring helps build the networks and skills that are vital to this responsive organization of the future.

Mentees as Organizational Learning Links

Mentees, whether involved in a formal program, an informal relationship with a mentor, or only occasional and sporadic mentoring, develop trust and even caring for those who have guided them. Organizations that treat mentoring as a way of life can capitalize on those relationships.

In the many-layered machine-age organization, conflict between management and labor was assumed. Therefore, in many companies and agencies workers were expected to "park their brains at the factory gate, do what they were told and keep their mouths shut"—hardly an environment to gain from employee know-how. Workers were also isolated from one another, and chatting among themselves was often punished.

In the information-age organization, the employer needs the knowledge, skill and ability of every employee to remain competitive, discover threats to the organization's future and design effective responses to those challenges.

In a growing number of organizations, a network of mentors and their mentees are forming to ensure that information gets to the right place and is combined with the right data to form the best possible response, whether the information is perceived as a threat or an opportunity. Thus, a mentor/mentee network of trusting, caring, sharing, and helping people ensures that the needs created by change are handled quickly.

EXERCISE

Describe how a network of mentors and mentees could be valuable to your organization.

_____

_____

_____

The Long Bottom Line

Organizations that encourage and train their people in the skills of mentoring may reap their rewards as long as those people are employed there. Organizations often benefit from their investment in mentoring for years, even decades, because of what has passed from mentor to mentee and back again.

Since real mentoring enhances mentee performance, avoids failures or mistakes, and encourages fresh ideas, the financial benefits to the employer can continue well into the future.

Some Points to Remember

➤ Mentoring tends to be most productive when it operates as an adult-to-adult partnership.

➤ The partnership is voluntary on both sides—even in formal, organization-sponsored programs. To be effective, both partners must be committed to it and willing to do their part.

➤ Mentees have a responsibility to manage their own development and career. They need to study and practice the skills that will foster a good mentoring relationship.

➤ Being mentored is not a training program and not an entitlement. Mentoring is the act of going above and beyond the ordinary to produce powerful, positive change in another person.

➤ Either party is entitled to terminate the relationship at any time, with or without giving a reason. But when effective partnerships have resulted in achieving the intended goals, gratitude and celebration are in order!

Remember: Mentors Help—Mentees Do!

Now Available From

CRISP PUBLICATIONS

Books•Videos•CD-ROMs•Computer-Based Training Products

If you enjoyed this book, we have great news for you. There are over 200 books available in the *50-Minute*™ Series. To request a free full-line catalog, contact your local distributor or Crisp Publications, Inc., 1200 Hamilton Court, Menlo Park, CA 94025. Our toll-free number is 800-442-7477. Visit our website at: http://www.crisp-pub.com.

Subject Areas Include:

Management

Human Resources

Communication Skills

Personal Development

Marketing/Sales

Organizational Development

Customer Service/Quality

Computer Skills

Small Business and Entrepreneurship

Adult Literacy and Learning

Life Planning and Retirement

CRISP WORLDWIDE DISTRIBUTION

English language books are distributed worldwide. Major international distributors include:

ASIA/PACIFIC

Australia/New Zealand: In Learning, PO Box 1051, Springwood QLD, Brisbane, Australia 4127   Tel: 61-7-3-841-2286, Facsimile: 61-7-3-841-1580
ATTN: Messrs. Gordon

Philippines: National Book Store Inc., Quad Alpha Centrum Bldg, 125 Pioneer Street, Mandaluyong, Metro Manila, Philippines   Tel: 632-631-8051, Facsimile: 632-631-5016

Singapore, Malaysia, Brunei, Indonesia: Times Book Shops. Direct sales HQ: STP Distributors, Pasir Panjang Distrientre, Block 1 #03-01A, Pasir Panjang Rd, Singapore 118480   Tel: 65-2767626, Facsimile: 65-2767119

Japan: Phoenix Associates Co., Ltd., Mizuho Bldng, 3-F, 2-12-2, Kami Osaki, Shinagawa-Ku, Tokyo 141   Tel: 81-33-443-7231, Facsimile: 81-33-443-7640
ATTN: Mr. Peter Owans

CANADA

Reid Publishing, Ltd., Box 69559, 60 Briarwood Avenue, Port Credit, Ontario, Canada L5G 3N6 Tel: (905) 842-4428, Facsimile: (905) 842-9327
ATTN: Mr. Steve Connolly/Mr. Jerry McNabb

Trade Book Stores: Raincoast Books, 8680 Cambie Street, Vancouver, B.C., V6P 6M9
Tel: (604) 323-7100, Facsimile: (604) 323-2600   ATTN: Order Desk

EUROPEAN UNION

England: Flex Training, Ltd., 9-15 Hitchin Street, Baldock, Hertfordshire, SG7 6A, England Tel: 44-1-46-289-6000, Facsimile: 44-1-46-289-2417
ATTN: Mr. David Willetts

INDIA

Multi-Media HRD, Pvt., Ltd., National House, Tulloch Road, Appolo Bunder, Bombay, India 400-039   Tel: 91-22-204-2281, Facsimile: 91-22-283-6478
ATTN: Messrs. Aggarwal

SOUTH AMERICA

Mexico: Grupo Editorial Iberoamerica, Nebraska 199, Col. Napoles, 03810 Mexico, D.F.
Tel: 525-523-0994, Facsimile: 525-543-1173   ATTN: Señor Nicholas Grepe

SOUTH AFRICA

Alternative Books, PO Box 1345, Ferndale 2160, South Africa
Tel: 27-11-792-7730, Facsimile: 27-11-792-7787   ATTN: Mr. Vernon de Haas

VER.A